WALKING WIDOWED

Reflections on a Loss

Pamela L. Goodness

Walking Widowed: Reflections on a Loss

Copyright © 2020 Pamela L. Goodness.

Produced and printed by Stillwater River Publications.

All rights reserved.

Written and produced in the United States of America.
This book may not be reproduced or sold in any form without the expressed, written permission of the author and publisher.

Visit our website at **www.StillwaterPress.com** for more information.

First Stillwater River Publications Edition

ISBN: 978-1-952521-23-2

Library of Congress Control Number: 2020910766

1 2 3 4 5 6 7 8 9 10
Written & illustrated by Pamela L. Goodness
Published by Stillwater River Publications
Pawtucket, RI, USA.

Publisher's Cataloging-In-Publication Data
    (Prepared by The Donohue Group, Inc.)

Names: Goodness, Pamela L., author, illustrator.
Title: Walking widowed : reflections on a loss / Pamela L. Goodness.
Description: First Stillwater River Publications edition. | Pawtucket, RI, USA : Stillwater River Publications, [2020]
Identifiers: ISBN 9781952521232
Subjects: LCSH: Widowhood--Poetry. | Grief--Poetry. | Bereavement--Poetry. | Goodness, Pamela L. | LCGFT: Poetry. | Biographies.
Classification: LCC PS3607.O592252 W35 2020 | DDC 811/.6--dc23

*The views and opinions expressed in this book
are solely those of the author and do not necessarily
reflect the views and opinions of the publisher.*

To my late husband Lee
forever my lover,
forever my friend,
forever loved.

Contents

The Journey	1
I Call Out Your Name	2
Grief in Random	3
Time	4
Companions	5
Exposed	6
Letting Go	7
You Carried My Lover Away	8
Life Interrupted	9
A Voice	10
Call It By Name	11
Forgive Me	12
Thirteen Months	14
I Speak Your Name	16
Confusion	17
Stars	18
Left Behind	19
In Flight	20
Fearless	21
Desire	22
You	23
Wrong Time, Wrong Place	24
Beautiful Day	25
I Celebrate You	26
He Waits for Me	27
A Previous Longing	28
Grief's Journey	29
Alight with Love	30
Broken	31
Remembrance	32
Acknowledgements	35
About the Author	36

THE JOURNEY

We call it a journey ... as if it's taken voluntarily
                 ... with anticipation of hours
                     filled with joy
                     ... with moments of great laughter
                     ... with memories to cherish

We call it a journey ... knowing we would never take
                     it voluntarily
                     ... it's fraught with relentless
                     torment
                     ... moments of terror
                     ... hours of overwhelming sadness
                     ... nights of haunting loneliness

Damn this journey!

I CALL OUT YOUR NAME

Love . . . sorrow, forever joined in your name.
My broken heart cries out your name.
Deep sadness . . . love everlasting, becomes your name.
I call out your name . . . silence returns.

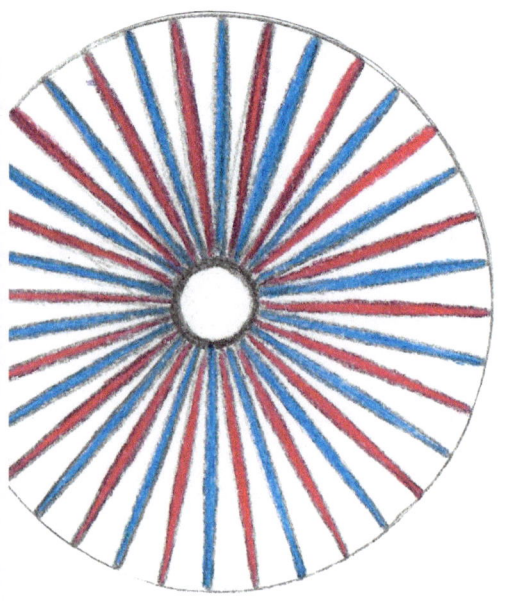

GRIEF IN RANDOM

Never thought I'd have to live in the world without you.
Never thought I'd be on my own,
    having to find my way . . .
        without you to carry me through the day.

You promised to live forever,
but promises never hold and I couldn't hold on to you.

Oh solitary soul,
what brought you to this journey,
and where you go . . . I do not know.

TIME

Time . . . you were the enemy
I knew it from the start.
You walked with me
You talked to me
You followed me close behind.
I told myself it was only in my mind . . .
    but
You caught up with me . . . when he and I were us.
You stalked us
Laughed at us . . . each year you gained on us.
Till one day . . . we lost the fight.

COMPANIONS

There you are
I thought you were deep ... deep down
Somewhere I couldn't find you
Somewhere you couldn't find me.
Then you appear and I know you are always there ... waiting.
Waiting ... for a word
        a memory
        a passage read
There you are ... just below the surface.
    ... filling my eyes with tears
        ... shattering my heart.
I think we shall always be together now
    Companions ... I reluctant, you ruthless.

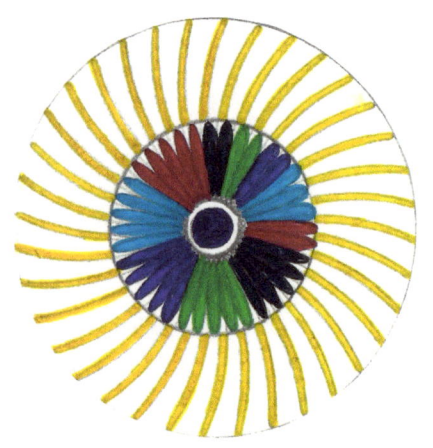

EXPOSED

The waves crash in, cover me,
   silken, they slip away . . .
      exposed . . . shivering.

Warm upon the sands, cover me,
   timeless, they slip away . . .
      exposed . . . shivering.

Sultry winds whipping 'round, cover me,
   hurry past, they slip away . . .
      exposed . . . shivering.

LETTING GO

Like a summer storm it came, carrying the threat of harm.
Passing, the summer sun shone again,
    lulling us into complacency.
Again and again it returned, buffeting us, leaving only
    minor damage... seeing the signs, we chose to ignore.

Years passed, the storms became more frequent,
    the damage more intense.
Still in denial... came the tsunami, sweeping away
    all that we knew... leaving only remnants of who
    you were... who we were together.

Heaving and straining against the relentless winds...
    denial was futile,
        tearing us apart and holding us together...
        battered and weary,
            letting go of the branch you clung to...
        I let go of you.

YOU CARRIED MY LOVER AWAY

You came like a blanket and covered me . . .
    when you carried my lover away.
Your blanket made of grief.
You wrapped it round me
    and
I pulled it tight against my skin . . .
    the only warmth I could find . . .
        after you carried my lover away.

LIFE INTERRUPTED

Holding hands
    Knowing glances
        Playful caresses
            Bodies entwined
Empty rooms
    Hours to fill
        Silence that echoes
            Body . . .

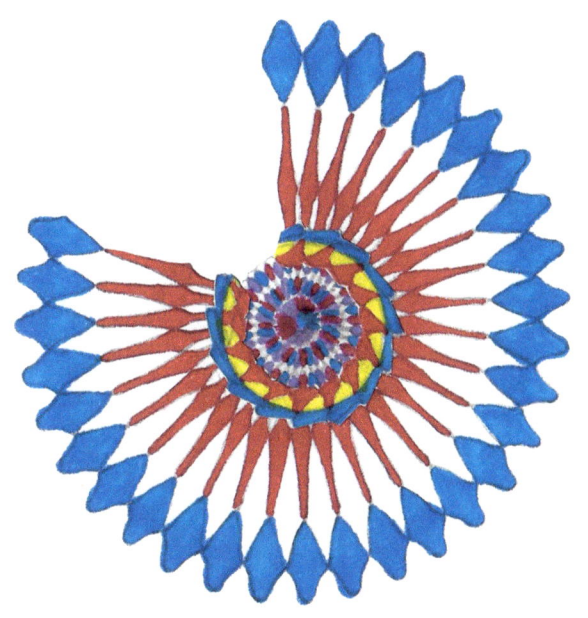

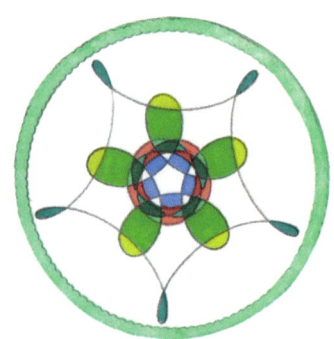

A VOICE

When at my lowest ebb
    and pain the deepest,
a voice ... so soothing that it sheltered,
      so strong that it inspired.
a voice ... filled with compassion ...
      ... understanding and hope,
    touched my heart ... reached through to my soul,
      and renewed in me,
        that life was still worth living.

CALL IT BY NAME

I could not bring myself to ask you . . . how it felt?
    If you were consumed by fear or full of regret.
    If you were resigned or even prepared.
I knew if I asked I would have to use that word . . .
    to bring it into the light,
    to bring it into our life.
I thought if we refrained from calling it by name . . .
    maybe it would take away its power,
    and deny it a presence in our life.
I could not bring myself to ask you . . . how it felt?
    because it was I who was consumed by fear
    and full of regret.

FORGIVE ME

I hope you can forgive me,
I had no idea,
 no concept,
  no sense ... how selfish I was.

You were trapped in your body ...
 what fears you may have had,
 what terror you might have felt,
 how great might the loneliness have been ...
  yet I stayed a distance away.

Not knowing how endless touch
 might have taken the fear away.
Not knowing how meaningless
 my words of solace must have sounded.

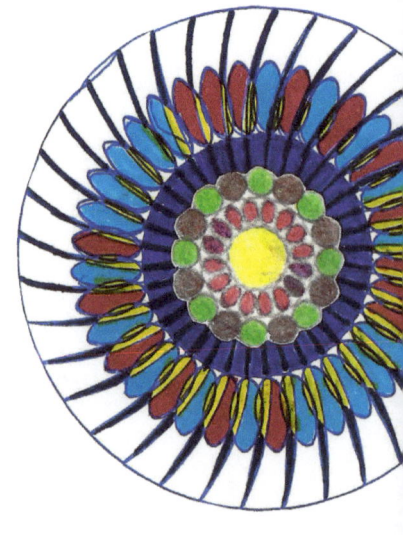

I didn't know . . .
    didn't understand . . .
        death was academic, despite it staring back at me.

I hope you can forgive me . . .
    for not holding you tighter,
    not touching you more deeply,
    for looking at you, but not seeing you,
    for not finding a way to keep you alive.

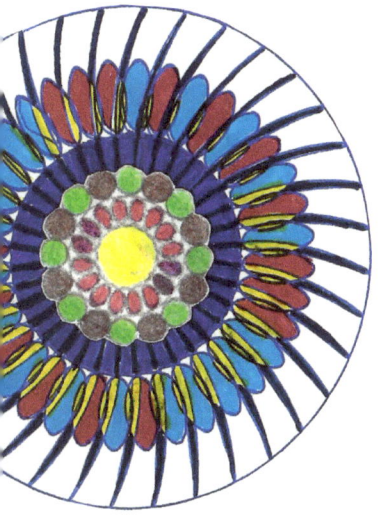

THIRTEEN MONTHS

Thirteen months and all that's left me is . . . without.
Thirteen months of living . . . without.
Thirteen months still reaching and expecting your hand
    to envelop mine . . .
    but all that's left me is . . . without.
Thirteen months . . . without you and a heart still broken.
Thirteen months . . . without you and I still don't know
    how to mend.
Thirteen months . . . without you and the days still feel
    empty, even when they are full.

Thirteen months . . . without . . .
Thirteen months . . . without,
    the words echo in my head
            . . . without your gentle touch.
            . . . without your comforting voice.
            . . . without your reassuring embrace.

Thirteen months . . . without waking to the warmth
   of your body.
      . . . without sleeping cradled safely in your arms.
      . . . without my head nestled in your chest, feeling your
         soft hairs caressing my thirsting lips.

Thirteen months and 'should' creeps into conversations,
   even as hot tears still pool in my red-rimmed eyes
   and run down the hollow of my cheeks.
Thirteen months and . . . 'should' is their word.
Thirteen months and 'without' is mine.

I SPEAK YOUR NAME

Lee . . . I speak your name aloud
    To keep you alive in the world
    Despite the fear I see in their eyes.

Lee . . . I speak your name aloud
    To keep open the door, that leads me back to you
    To hear it again in my voice
    To feel it again upon my lips.

Lee . . . I speak your name aloud
    To keep you alive in me.

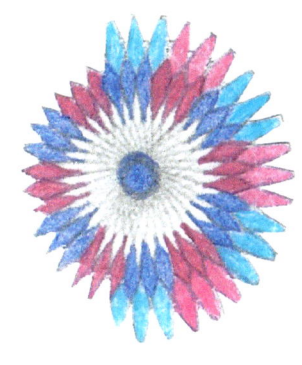

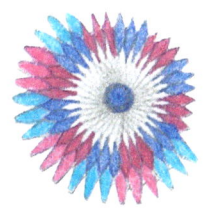

CONFUSION

Of the world I wonder . . .
Many questions,
Too few answers,
    lost love?
    love everlasting?
I wander weary
Seeking . . . finding . . . falling
    loss again,
    lost again.
Want waining,
    Hurry forward.
Step back slowly,
    Confusion prevails.

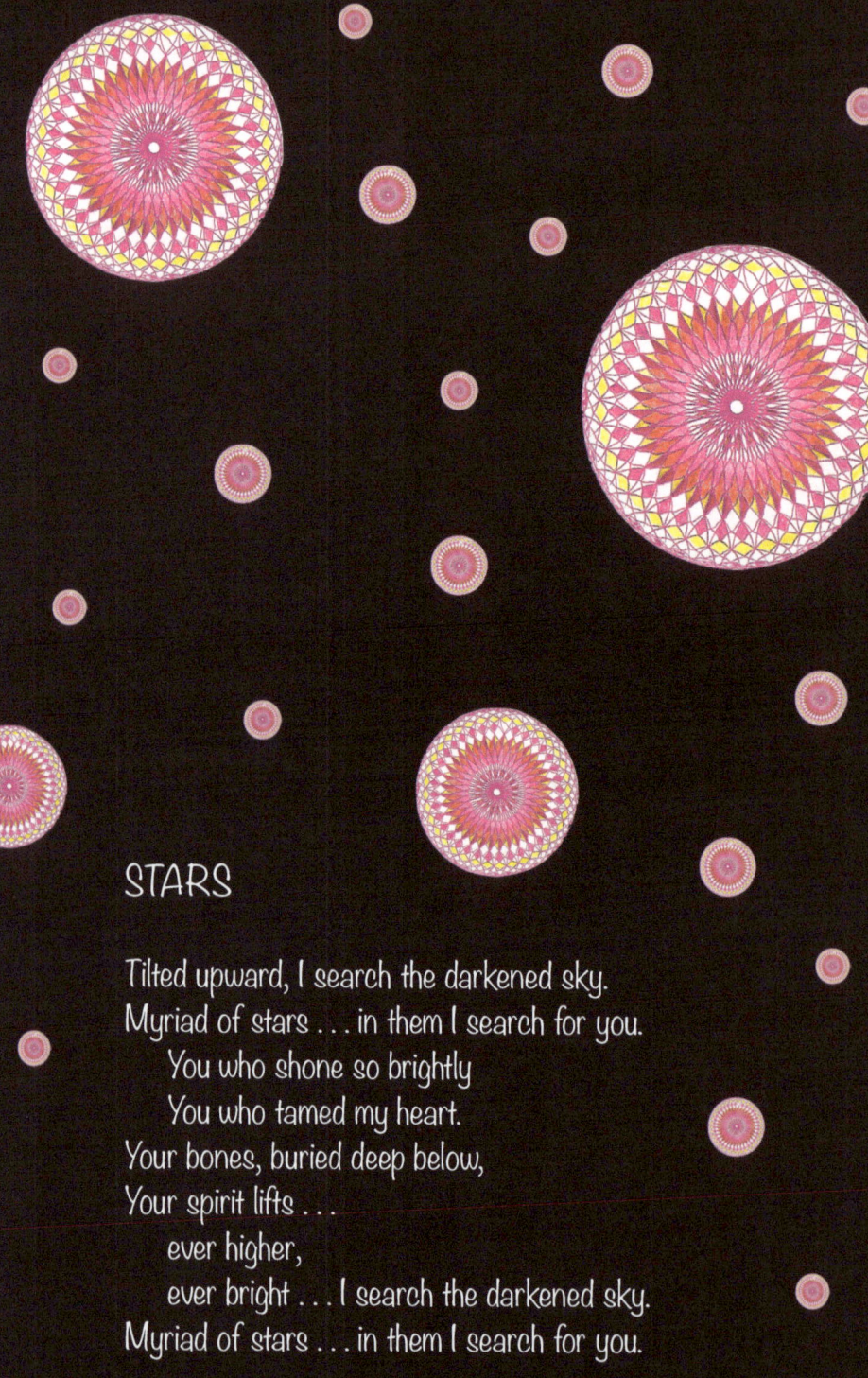

STARS

Tilted upward, I search the darkened sky.
Myriad of stars … in them I search for you.
    You who shone so brightly
    You who tamed my heart.
Your bones, buried deep below,
Your spirit lifts …
    ever higher,
    ever bright … I search the darkened sky.
Myriad of stars … in them I search for you.

LEFT BEHIND

Left behind, but not forgotten
You visit me each night . . .
Kissing me often . . . holding me tight.
Together again . . . we talk
               . . . we laugh
               . . . we even fight.
By day you're out of sight,
But having you near . . . each night,
As you hold me tight,
My memories take flight!

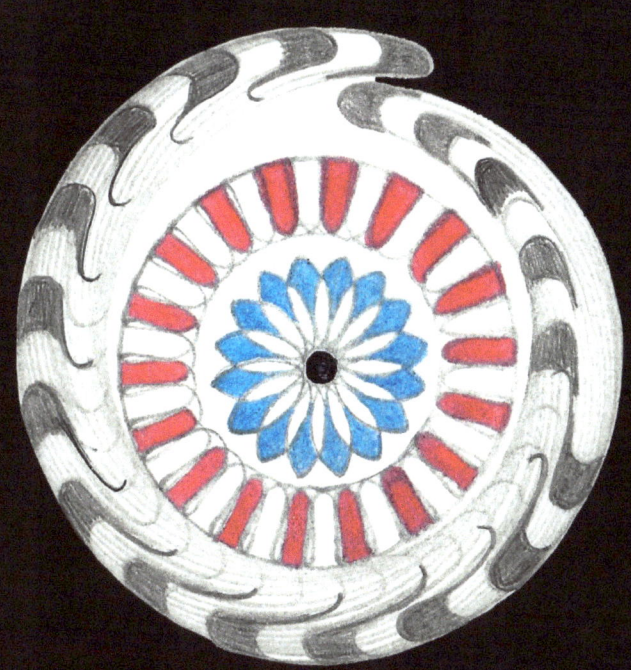

IN FLIGHT

I see you in the birds in flight,
    upon the currents you soar ... swooping low,
        winging on high ... no longer tethered.

Boundless and free,
    upon the winds you drift ...
        among the clouds by day ...
            by night among the stars.

FEARLESS

You, who knew how to live life better than I...

    You, who were courageous, curious, craving adventure...

        You, who were fearless.

I, who stood back fearful to venture, frightened to try...

    I would have given you my future... had I the chance,

        You, who would make better use of it.

DESIRE

You were my heart's desire
    In you I found my fire
Never did I tire, of the voice that inspired . . .
    or the touch that required . . . my touch in return.
You were my heart's desire
    Caused me to reach higher
Your leaving has not extinguished the desire
    Only the fire . . . broken on the funeral pyre.

YOU

You lay there on the counter mocking me,
    reminding me how alone I am.
You, so very small ... your message so big, is undeniable.

Each time I look at you, my thoughts rush back to a day ...
    laughing, we pull you apart, our wishes ready.

Now upon the counter you lay,
    no two hands for grasping,
    no two hands to pull you apart.

All that's left me is a silent wish ... you cannot grant.

WRONG TIME, WRONG PLACE

Just too lonely,
    feeling unloved.

You came along,
    wrong time, wrong place.

Can't deny the feelings,
    can't show them either.

Hold it together,
    hold it all back.

Maybe it's just too lonely,
    but I know it's real.

BEAUTIFUL DAY

Sun dappled leaves,
Reflections on water,
Warm summer breezes . . .
    remind me, that I'm missing you.

Squirrels foraging,
Children frolicking,
Lovers nestled on blankets . . .
    remind me, that I'm missing you.

Wistful smiles,
Whispered words,
Hands entwined . . .
    remind me, that I'm missing you.

Beautiful day,
Beckons me forward,
Out of the shadows . . .
    only to remind me, that I'm missing you.

I CELEBRATE YOU

Energized, my heart pours out the words
    my soul endeavors to claim.
Tonight my restlessness cannot be curbed or contained.
Tonight you join me,
    as I celebrate you,
    rejoice in you,
    return to you.

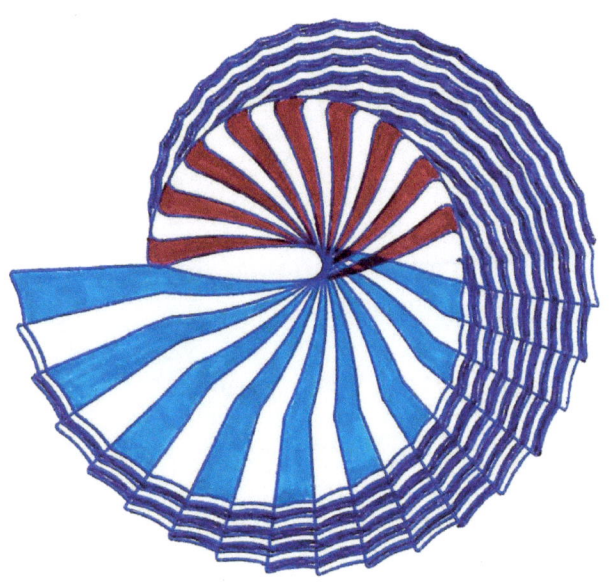

HE WAITS FOR ME

He waits for me, so
I do not fear you . . . as once I did.
You hold no menace,
Your cruelty holds no sway,
The oblivion you threaten no longer frightens me.

He waits for me, so
I ask only . . . come quietly . . . as you did for him.
No need for tumult,
Only our embrace . . .
In that place . . .
Where time no longer holds.

A PREVIOUS LONGING

Life, precise in its order,
    mess at a minimum,
        Each step measured,
            its outcome predictable.
A previous longing,
    now in fruition,
        now to regret.

GRIEF'S JOURNEY

TEARS
Overwhelming ... grief
   panicked ... thoughts
Utter ... despair
   desperate ... loneliness
TEARS
Endless ... longing
   blinding ... fear
Crushing ... sadness
   bits of ... laughter
TEARS
Moments of ... peace
   sweetest of memories
Begrudging resignation
   reluctant acceptance

ALIGHT WITH LOVE

Lights flicker in bags alight with love.
    Each a broken heart,
    Each a cherished memory, a secret held.

Lights flicker in bags alight with love.
    Unbroken circle, casting shadows,
    connecting lives, strangers meet
        as
Lights flicker in bags alight with love.
    Strength in numbers, hand in hand,
    hearts begin to mend.
    Pain's grip loosens,
    a lightness of being returns
        as
Lights flicker in bags alight with love.

BROKEN

Broken pieces,
Broken heart.
Against my will, I begin to mend.
Tears once hot, now run cool,
　　fear subsides, lost joy returns.
Stolen moments . . . peace arrives.
I've found a place for you to rest . . .
　　in my still broken heart.

REMEMBRANCE

A sacred space,
   angelic voices raised in
      songs of love and loss…
         we gather together to remember them.

Outside, darkness rises, cold descends,
      inside, words of love, a common bond, warm us,
         as we gather together to remember them.

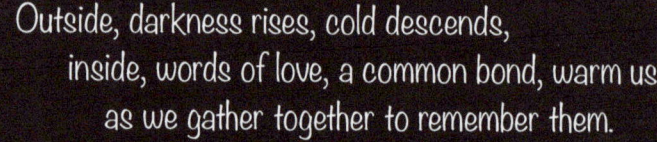

Carrying the broken pieces, strewn about our lives…
      the pain of missing, the fear of loss,
         the weight of remembrance…
            we gather together to remember them.

In the stillness comes the gentle fall of winter's snow,
      a blanket of white to cover the pain,
         as we gather together to remember them.

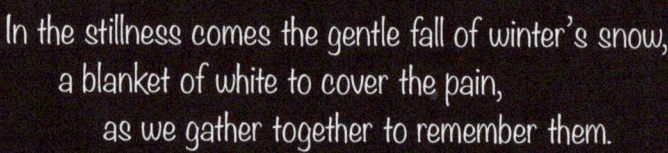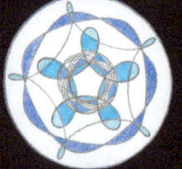

Photography Credits

Page 30: 'Luminaires' at A Weekend of Hope and Healing Adult Retreat—
HopeHealth Hospice & Palliative Care.

Page 33: Light Up A Life: A Time For Remembrance—
HopeHealth Hospice & Palliative Care.

Acknowledgements

To Guy Murgo, an extraordinary mentor and cherished friend, without whose compassion, support, and encouragement I would never have had the courage to expose my heart and put these words to paper.

To Joanne Olson my treasured lifetime friend, whose love and support has enabled me to venture out of my comfort zone many times throughout my life.

To my family, friends, and the people of HopeHealth Hospice and Palliative Care, all of whom helped me, after the death of my husband, to overcome despair and find new meaning in my life.

To Steven and Dawn Porter and Emma St. Jean of Stillwater River Publishing Co. for for their outstanding work in bringing to fruition my lifelong dream of seeing my poetry in print.

About the Author
Pamela L. Goodness

A resident of Smithfield, Rhode Island. A graduate of Rhode Island College, University of Rhode Island, and Salve Regina University. A retired educator and school librarian for 24 years and now an enthusiastic volunteer at HopeHealth Hospice and Palliative Care. This is her first published collection of poems.

www.ingramcontent.com/pod-product-compliance
Lightning Source LLC
Chambersburg PA
CBHW041527090426
42736CB00035B/34